Managing Editor
Mara Ellen Guckian

Editor in Chief
Karen J. Goldfluss, M.S. Ed.

Creative Director
Sarah M. Fournier

Cover Artist
Diem Pascarella

Illustrator
Tom McKee

Art Coordinator
Renée Mc Elwee

Imaging
Amanda R. Harter

Publisher
Mary D. Smith, M.S. Ed.

Author

Jessica Franzene

Teacher Created Resources
12621 Western Avenue
Garden Grove, CA 92841
www.teachercreated.com

ISBN: 978-1-4206-8109-3

©2018 Teacher Created Resources
Reprinted, 2019
Made in U.S.A.

Table of Contents

Introduction

Reading and Writing Activities for Social-Emotional Learning includes 15 units revolving around character development. The units were designed to help students develop a strong set of social and emotional skills necessary to cope with the social aspects of their daily lives. After reading each passage, students are provided with four different writing activities to gauge their understanding of the concepts provided.

Units can be presented consecutively or used as needed to address specific situations. Each unit is set up in the same manner and includes the following components:

- **Teacher Notes** — Designed for the busy teacher, this page summarizes the passage and highlights the concepts addressed. Three or four thought-provoking discussion questions are provided for each reading passage. These questions should help guide the teacher when presenting each unit.

- **Reading Passage** — Each 3-page reading passage addresses a different aspect of character development in an age-appropriate manner. These passages can be read independently by students or as shared reading in small groups. (See page 4 for Lexile Level Chart.)

Many passages describe contemporary situations and how the characters may or may not deal with them. When possible, these passages leave it up to the student to determine how the characters resolved the situations they found themselves in. Other passages discuss events in history and how people's actions changed the way citizens were treated.

- **Reading Comprehension Questions** — Five questions follow each reading passage. The questions were designed to assess students' understanding of what they read. By reviewing these questions and answers as a class, educators can readily assess if students are grasping the material presented. These questions will hopefully be used as conversation starters to discuss the topics in greater depth when appropriate.

- **Writing Activities** — Four different writing activities are provided in each unit to increase understanding of each character development topic. Hopefully there will be time available for each activity, but if not, teachers may choose which activities are most appropriate for their students. These writing activities include poems, letter writing, journal entries, diary entries, and more.

Lexile Level Chart

Unit/Passage Title	Page	Lexile	Word Count
Unit 1—Appreciation	6	530	412
Unit 2—Caring	14	540	427
Unit 3—Citizenship	22	490	416
Unit 4—Courage	30	510	406
Unit 5—Fairness	38	530	354
Unit 6—Generosity	46	520	423
Unit 7—Good Judgment	54	510	443
Unit 8—Honesty	62	530	375
Unit 9—Loyalty	70	520	405
Unit 10—Patriotism	78	520	423
Unit 11—Perseverance	86	500	399
Unit 12—Respect	94	540	433
Unit 13—Responsibility	102	530	434
Unit 14—Tolerance	110	520	432
Unit 15—Trustworthiness	118	510	396

Learning About . . .
Appreciation

Teacher Notes

Passage Summary

Mrs. Garcia's students throw her a retirement party, and some of her former students attend to show their appreciation for her hard work and thoughtfulness during her career.

Concepts to Consider

The children in Mrs. Garcia's class know that she is a good, caring teacher, and they want to show her how much she is appreciated. When her former students show up, it gives the kids a glimpse of the big picture of the teacher's career, and a chance to grasp how much her guidance and affection means in the long run. Instead of taking a good teacher for granted, both the children and adults in the story take the time to let Mrs. Garcia know how much they appreciate her effort and dedication. Another aspect of appreciation in the story is Mrs. Garcia's appreciation of the kids' party and the adults' contributions.

Discussion Questions

- How do you think Mrs. Garcia felt about the party? Why do you think so?

- What do you think was Mrs. Garcia's favorite thing about the party: the snacks, the decorations, the presents, or what people said about her? Why do you think so?

- Tell about a time when you showed someone how much you appreciated him or her.

Shannon was hanging the homemade sign. José was blowing up the balloons. Frankie was putting the snacks on the table. The other kids were busy, too. They were watching for Mrs. Garcia to come down the hall.

"Here she comes," Andrea whispered. Whew! The kids had finished just in time.

They all ran to their desks and sat quietly. Their hearts were pounding with excitement.

It seemed like a very long time until Mrs. Garcia finally opened the classroom door.

"Good morning, children," she said. Then she saw the decorations and the balloons. She was so surprised! The kids were thrilled that she hadn't guessed about the party.

"My goodness," Mrs. Garcia said. "What is all this?"

Page 1

Appreciation

"It's a party for you," said Andrea. "We heard you will be done teaching this year. We wanted to thank you for all the things you've done for us."

"And for us, too."

Everyone in the class turned to see who had said that. The kids were just as surprised as Mrs. Garcia when a bunch of grown-ups came into the classroom.

"It's wonderful to see you!" said Mrs. Garcia. Then she told the kids, "They are from the first class I ever taught. That was more than 30 years ago."

"We heard about the party, and we wanted to say 'thank you,' too," said one of the men.

The grown-ups came inside the classroom. Some of them were holding presents.

"Is it all right if we tell your students stories about when you were our teacher?" a woman asked Mrs. Garcia.

Page 2

Mrs. Garcia still looked surprised. "Of course," she said.

One of the men said, "I had Mrs. Garcia in the first grade. She helped me after school every single day, because I had trouble learning the alphabet."

Another man said, "Mrs. Garcia knew that I wanted to be a doctor when i grew up. She helped me learn about science. Today, I am a doctor. If she hadn't helped me, I might not have become one."

A woman told the class, "The other kids used to tease me because I was different. Mrs. Garcia told me that I was special, not different. She made me feel good about myself."

As other grown-ups told about Mrs. Garcia, the kids realized that she still did the same things to help kids. She made them feel special. She helped them learn. The kids were glad they had shown Mrs. Garcia how much they all appreciated her.

Page 3

Name: _____

1 **What <u>two</u> things did the students do to get ready for the party?**

   a) blew up balloons

   b) made a cake

   c) hung a sign

   d) wrote a card

2 **True or false? Mrs. Garcia has been a teacher for more than 15 years.**

   a) true   b) false

3 **What is the main idea of the story?**

   a) Mrs. Garcia has been teaching a long time.

   b) Mrs. Garcia's class throws her a surprise party to show they appreciate her.

   c) Mrs. Garcia makes people feel special.

   d) Mrs. Garcia's class was excited to throw her a party.

4 **What does it mean to "appreciate" someone?**

   a) You think they are exciting.

   b) You are grateful for things they do.

   c) You pay them money you owe them.

   d) You think they are nice.

5 **Do the students like or dislike Mrs. Garcia? Tell why you think so.**

   _____

   _____

   _____

   _____

   _____

A Imagine that Mrs. Garcia was your teacher. Write her a letter to thank her for helping you. Include some ways in which she helped.

_____

_____

_____

_____

_____

_____

_____

_____

_____

_____

Name: _____

B What might the children have written on the sign they made for Mrs. Garcia? Think of three ideas. Write about them in the box below.

C Write about a time when someone helped you, and how you showed, or could have shown, your appreciation.

_____

_____

_____

_____

_____

_____

D Work with a partner to think of three ways in which people can show their appreciation for one another. Write your ideas below, and share them with others.

I Appreciate You!

1 _____

_____

_____

_____

2 _____

_____

_____

_____

3 _____

_____

_____

_____

Teacher Notes

Passage Summary

Mother Teresa spends her entire adult life ministering to the needs of the "poorest of the poor."

Concepts to Consider

Mother Teresa is a prime example of someone who personified the word "caring." Her self-sacrifice is legendary, but her determination to persist in her efforts in the face of poverty is perhaps the most inspirational part of her story. She truly cared about all people, and inspired thousands, if not millions, of others to give both time and money to lift others up.

Discussion Questions

- What are some ways that Mother Teresa showed caring?

- Mother Teresa knew she couldn't help everyone, but she decided to help as many people as she could. Do you think that was a good idea? Why or why not?

- Why do you think other people followed her example?

- How do you think people felt when Mother Teresa helped them?

Mother Teresa was not really a mother. She never had children of her own. When she was a very young girl, she decided that she wanted to make sick people feel better. She wanted to help people that others had forgotten about. She called them "the poorest of the poor." She could not stop thinking about ways to help them—they needed food, they needed medicine, and they needed someone to love them. She became a loving mother to thousands of people who needed her.

Mother Teresa worked hard every day and night. It was hard to get enough sleep. Sometimes, she got sick. But even when she felt tired or sick, she kept working. She helped poor and sick people as much as she could. This was because she knew they felt worse than she did.

Page 1

She lived in a place that had many poor people who were sick and hungry. Mother Teresa had a plan. She would do what she could for them. She would also set a good example, so that other people would help.

People did see what Mother Teresa was doing to help the sick and the poor. They saw that she cared about them more than she did about herself. She would hold sick people in her arms and make them feel better.

Years passed. Mother Teresa was getting weaker, but many other good people had joined her in helping the poor. They assisted old and young people. They started schools. They gave medicine and healthy food to families. They helped people who were blind. They looked after those who could not walk.

Sometimes, Mother Teresa felt sad that she could not make everyone feel better. There were so many people who needed her! How could she ever help them all?

Page 2

Others told her that she should be proud of all she had done. She even got awards and medals for her work. People all over the world knew her name. They thought she was a wonderful person.

However, Mother Teresa did not care about being famous. She did not care about the medals. In fact, she didn't want to own things. Once, a man gave her a special car. He wanted her to use it for herself. Mother Teresa had a contest. She sold tickets and gave the car away as the prize. She used the money to open a place for sick people to live.

Mother Teresa died in 1997. She had spent most of her life helping others. She is remembered for all the good things she did.

Page 3

1 **What made Mother Teresa sad?**

　a)　She was sick.

　b)　Other people were helping poor people.

　c)　There were so many people who needed help.

　d)　She was not famous.

2 **What were some things that Mother Teresa and others did to help poor people?**

_____

_____

_____

3 **True or false? Mother Teresa's children helped care for people.**

　a)　true

　b)　false

4 **What does the word "weaker" mean?**

　a)　not being as strong

　b)　feeling happier

　c)　able to do more

　d)　on a set schedule

5 **What did Mother Teresa do with the car she was given?**

　a)　She drove it to another country.

　b)　She sold it for food for herself.

　c)　She used it to raise money to build a home for sick people.

　d)　She gave it to poor people.

Name: _____

A Write about a time when you were tired or sick, but you helped someone who felt worse than you did.

_____

_____

_____

_____

_____

_____

_____

_____

_____

_____

Name: _____

B Imagine you are Mother Teresa. Write a diary entry about a day in your life.

Dear Diary,

_____

_____

_____

_____

_____

C Write about a time when someone acted in a caring way toward you. Explain what that meant to you.

_____

_____

_____

_____

_____

_____

Name: _____

D Pretend that you are one of the people that Mother Teresa helped. Write her a thank-you note.

_____

_____

_____

_____

_____

_____

_____

_____

_____

_____

Teacher Notes

Passage Summary

Jamie learns that even a little bit of litter hurts, and even a little bit of volunteering helps.

Concepts to Consider

In this story, Jamie is initially reluctant to volunteer, partially because he doesn't think litter is his problem, and partially because he would rather do something else. As he participates in making his community a better place, he sees his efforts help both animals and people. He acknowledges that those who litter are doing wrong, but doesn't dwell on the value judgment. Rather, he focuses on what he can do to undo the wrong. His reward isn't material, but he is satisfied that his efforts are acknowledged and plans to do even more. The adults in the story do not need to guide him to his conclusions—he simply needed an opportunity to participate in a positive way, and then he came to the realization on his own.

Discussion Questions

- How did Jamie make the park a better place for animals and for people?

- How will Jamie act the next time he sees someone litter?

- Have you ever changed your mind about something that you first thought didn't matter?

"Let's see," Mr. Dylan said. "We've got our orange vests, our gloves, and our trash bags. I think we're ready."

"What a dumb idea for a field trip," Jamie whispered to Hector. "I can't believe that we have to pick up someone else's garbage."

Hector whispered back, "At least we won't be stuck inside all day."

Jamie had to admit that was true. It was nice and sunny out. It might be fun to go to the nature park. Still, spending a whole day looking for litter didn't seem like fun. Jamie didn't litter—well, not very much anyway. Why should he have to clean up somebody else's mess?

The bus dropped them off at the park gates. Mr. Dylan handed each kid a pair of gloves and a bag.

"Did I mention there's a prize for the student who picks up the most trash?" he said.

Jamie liked the sound of that. He pulled his gloves on and followed the other kids along the path.

Page 1

As he walked, he noticed cans, bottles, and wrappers on the ground. He was surprised there was so much trash.

"Do a lot of people come here?" he asked Mr. Dylan.

"Yes. It's hard for the workers to keep the place clean," Mr. Dylan said. "That's why they are happy when volunteers help."

Jamie listened to birds sing as he picked up litter. Squirrels jumped from branch to branch. Jamie even saw a rabbit sitting under a tree. He wondered what the animals thought of people. First, some people came to their home and dropped all this garbage. Then other people came along and cleaned it up. The animals probably think we are weird, he thought.

Page 2

By lunchtime, Jamie's bag was almost full. After the kids washed their hands, they sat down for a picnic. A park worker came by to thank them for helping.

"Let's see who wins the prize," the worker said. She checked the bags and said, "I think it's a tie." She pointed to Hector and Jamie.

"What's the prize?" Hector asked.

The worker smiled. "We will put your names on a sign in the park. The sign will say, 'Thank you for helping keep this place clean and safe for people and animals.'"

Jamie couldn't wait to come back and see the sign. He felt proud of what his class had accomplished. He decided that when he came back, he would bring a bag and gloves with him and pick up litter along the way.

Page 3

1 Choose <u>two</u> items the kids used to clean up litter.

    a)   grocery bags

    b)   gloves

    c)   trash bags

    d)   green vests

2 *Littering is wrong.* Is this a fact or an opinion? Explain your answer.

    a)   fact   b)   opinion

_____

_____

3 Do you think Jamie changed his mind about picking up litter by the end of the story? Why do you think that?

_____

_____

_____

4 The kids picked up litter. How did it get there in the first place?

    a)   They tossed it on the ground.

    b)   The animals left it there.

    c)   Other people threw it there while they were in the park.

    d)   The wind blew it there from the school.

5 Put the events of the story in order: _____   _____   _____   _____

    a)   ate a picnic lunch

    b)   rode the bus to the park

    c)   won the prize for picking up the most litter

    d)   picked up litter

A Imagine you are going on a picnic. Write a list of things you will do to leave the picnic area cleaner than when you got there.

My Picnic Plan

_____

_____

_____

_____

_____

_____

_____

_____

_____

_____

_____

Name: _____

B Write a poem about why you think it is important not to litter.

_____

_____

_____

_____

_____

C Write about a place you could help make cleaner. Explain how you would do it.

_____

_____

_____

_____

_____

Name: _____

D Write three things that a person can do to be a better citizen.

1 _____

_____

_____

_____

_____

2 _____

_____

_____

_____

_____

3 _____

_____

_____

_____

Teacher Notes

Passage Summary

Rosa Parks overcomes her fear and acts courageously, which helps other people be brave as well. The Civil Rights Movement is sparked by her act.

Concepts to Consider

Being brave is a lot harder if you are afraid, and children should be proud when they can overcome their fears. Rosa Parks acted alone, knowing the consequences would be harsh. Could she have imagined her act of defiance and bravery would have sparked the movement that brought segregation to an end? It also might be warranted to note to children that when Rosa Parks broke the law, it was a justified act because the law itself was unjust.

Discussion Questions

- What did Rosa Parks do that was brave?
- What happened after Rosa refused to give up her seat?
- Describe a time when you were brave.

Courage

Some people say courage means doing something you are afraid to do. Maybe you are afraid of what people will say. Maybe you are afraid that you will get into trouble. Either way, if you are afraid to do something you know is the right thing to do, but you find a way to do it, you are brave. And sometimes, if you are brave, it helps other people be brave, too.

In 1955, Rosa Parks helped other people be brave. Back then, black people had to do what white people said. Rosa was black. She rode a bus to work every day. One day, a white man told her he wanted to sit where she was sitting. The bus driver told her she had to move. Rosa was tired. She didn't think it was fair that she had to move because her skin was a different color. She did not get out of her seat for the man.

Page 1

Do you think that Rosa was afraid? She knew she was breaking a rule. She knew she could get into big trouble. And she did. Rosa got arrested.

Both black and white people heard about what Rosa had done. It made everyone think. Some people were angry that she had broken a rule, but some people thought she was very brave for breaking a rule that wasn't fair. Some thought she was just stirring up trouble.

Most importantly, many people decided that Rosa was right. They wanted to show others that they agreed with her. The city had made the law about black people giving up their seats to white people. The city owned the buses and made money from them. What if black people stopped riding the buses and walked instead? The city would lose money. Maybe the city would change the law then.

Page 2

Many black people decided to stop riding the buses. They walked to work and to the store. They found other ways to get places. For 382 days, they refused to ride the buses.

Finally, the city gave in. They changed the rule. Black people didn't have to give up their seats on buses anymore.

Rosa Parks was glad she had found the courage to stay in her seat on the bus that day. Her courage showed other people you could change the world. She knew that being afraid is part of being brave. She was happy that other people found courage, too.

Page 3

1 **What is another word for "courage"?**

    a) happiness

    b) belief

    c) fright

    d) bravery

2 **Why did Rosa get in trouble?**

    a) She stopped riding the buses.

    b) She told people to stop riding the buses.

    c) She would not give up her seat to a white man.

    d) She refused to get off the bus.

3 **Many people believed Rosa was right and the law should be changed. What did they do?**

    a) They stopped going to work.

    b) They stopped riding the buses.

    c) They bought their own buses.

    d) They paid extra to ride special buses.

4 **How long did people refuse to ride on buses?**

    a) 382 days

    b) one year

    c) nine months

    d) 328 days

5 *Rosa's courage helped change a law.* **Is this a fact or an opinion? Explain your answer.**

    a) fact   b) opinion

_____

_____

_____

Name: _____

A Imagine you are Rosa Parks. Write a letter to a friend explaining why you decided not to give up your seat.

_____

_____

_____

_____

_____

_____

_____

_____

_____

Name: _____

B Write about a time when you have shown courage. What did you do? How did you feel?

_____

_____

_____

_____

_____

C Write about a time when you helped someone else be brave. What did the person do? How did you feel?

_____

_____

_____

_____

_____

Name: _____

D Imagine you were on the bus with Rosa Parks when she refused to give up her seat. Write a journal entry to describe how you felt. Add a picture in the box below if you wish.

Dear Journal,

Today, _____

_____

_____

_____

_____

_____

_____

Unit 5

Teacher Notes

Passage Summary

Women, including Elizabeth Cady Stanton and Lucretia Mott, convene to make a plan to fight for the right to vote, as well as a host of other equal rights demands.

Concepts to Consider

Children tend to be taught that fairness exists throughout their world, and they sometimes have trouble conceptualizing what unfairness looks like, especially on a societal scale. The idea that women were treated as second-class citizens in the United States can be a startling one, but it is a useful example of how unfairness can be remedied. It is interesting to note that the change came from protest, as well as the persistence of the people protesting.

Discussion Questions

- How would you feel if you were not allowed to vote when you grow up?

- What are some reasons people didn't want women to vote? How do you feel about those reasons?

- What would it feel like to be one of the first women to vote?

One thing adults can do that kids cannot is vote. When you vote, you help choose who is in charge of your city, your state, and even your country. But did you know that for a long time, only certain adults were allowed to vote?

Years ago, women were not allowed to vote. Some people thought women were not as smart as men, so only men were allowed to vote. If women tried, they could be put in jail. These people were worried that women would not understand whom to vote for. They thought women should stay at home and let the men take care of everything.

Of course, most women were angry that they could not vote. Women were just as smart as men were. They should help decide who won elections.

Page 1

Instead of just being angry about the law, some women decided to fight for their rights. They tried to come up with ways to change the law. They formed groups and gave speeches. Sometimes they marched with signs.

Some women talked to their families about the law. They tried to explain to their husbands, fathers, and brothers that the rule was unfair. Some men agreed. But many did not.

The women had a big meeting to think of more ways to get the right to vote. Two women—Elizabeth Cady Stanton and Lucretia Mott —were in charge of the meeting.

Page 2

At the meeting, they wrote down what they wanted. They wanted women to have the same kinds of jobs as men. They wanted women and men to be paid the same. They wanted women to be able to go to any school they wanted. Of course, they also wanted women to vote.

Newspaper reporters heard about the meeting. They wrote stories about it in the papers. At first, people thought the women's ideas were bad. Later, more women and men thought about the ideas. They started to agree with them.

Finally, just about everyone agreed that women should be able to vote. The law was finally changed. The women had worked hard to be treated fairly, and they won rights that were equal to men's.

Name: _____

1 **What does "equal" mean?**

   a)   different

   b)   bigger

   c)   smaller

   d)   the same

2 **List four rights that women wanted.**

   • _____

   • _____

   • _____

   • _____

3 **List three things that women did to fight for their rights.**

   • _____

   • _____

   • _____

4 *Women are not as smart as men.* **Is this a fact or an opinion? Explain your answer.**

   a)   fact   b)   opinion

   _____

   _____

5 **Why do you think the women in the story were able to get the law changed?**

   _____

   _____

Name: _____

A Imagine your class is told that they can't play outside anymore. You know that this rule is not fair. What are three things you could do to help change this new rule? Think about what the women in the story did.

1 _____

_____

_____

_____

2 _____

_____

_____

_____

3 _____

_____

_____

_____

Name: _____

B What are three things you can use today to share your ideas that the women in the story did not have?

1 _____

2 _____

3 _____

C Write about a time when you helped make something fair.

_____

_____

_____

_____

_____

_____

_____

_____

Name: _____

D Write about something you do not think is fair. Explain why it is not fair. Then describe how it could be made fair.

I do not think it is fair that _____

_____

_____

_____

It is not fair because _____

_____

_____

_____

It would be fair if _____

_____

_____

_____

Teacher Notes

Passage Summary

Kara is excited about her birthday party, especially the presents she will get. During a trip to the store, she learns about food pantries and wonders what she can do to help needy families.

Concepts to Consider

Kara is neither greedy nor selfish to want stuffed animals for her birthday. Her implied decision to forego presents for herself is not so much a change of heart as a change in priorities. It is important to note that she was not aware of the existence of food pantries (and therefore needy families), and once she becomes aware, Kara immediately sets out to find a way to help. Sacrificing her potential presents is an act of simple generosity. It is interesting to note that one can be generous without actually being the giver—Kara isn't directly contributing to the food pantry, but is creatively trading a chance at material gain for the chance to make a difference. The story is open-ended, but the strong implication is that Kara will request food donations instead of presents.

Discussion Questions

- What kind of people do you think need help from a food pantry?
- Have you ever given up a chance to get something for yourself? Talk about it.
- How did Kara's mom change Kara's original plans for the party?
- Do you think Kara's mom knew Kara might change her plan if she learned about food pantries? Why do you think so?

"I want red and yellow balloons," Kara told her mother. "Oh, and can I have yellow candles on my cake?"

Mom smiled and wrote it down. She'd been adding notes to Kara's birthday party list for weeks.

Kara was having nine kids over because she would be nine years old. They would eat chocolate cake, drink red punch, and play games. This would be Kara's first big birthday party. It would be fun to have lots of kids running around and playing games, but Kara was especially excited about the presents. She hoped her guests would bring her stuffed animals. Kara collected them. She had hinted to her friends that she wanted more stuffed animals for her birthday. She needed more dogs and monkeys, and maybe a teddy bear or two.

Later that day, Kara and her mother went to the store to buy invitations for the party. Kara was puzzled when she saw her mother pick up several cans of soup and add them to her basket.

Page 1

"What's the soup for?" Kara asked.

"I'll show you on the way out," her mom said.

As they left the checkout line, Kara's mom handed her the bag of soup cans and pointed to a big box by the door. It had a sign on it that said "Food Pantry Donations."

"What's a food pantry?" Kara wondered aloud. She set the soup in the box and followed her mom outside.

"It's a place that gives food to people who can't afford to buy it," her mother explained.

Kara tried to imagine what that would be like. "Who doesn't have enough money for food?" she asked as they got in the car.

Page 2

"Well," her mom said, "some people lose their jobs or are too sick to work. They spend all their money just paying the bills. Then they do not have any money left to buy food. Some people can only buy a little food. They go to the food pantry to get more. Then they can feed their whole family."

Kara thought the whole way home. How could she help feed a family? She wanted to give to the food pantry, but not just a few cans of soup. Her allowance wasn't very much. Kara wanted to bring a lot of food to the pantry.

Suddenly, she had the answer.

That night, Kara finished her party invitations. On each one, she wrote a note about what she wanted for a gift. Presents like this would help many people. Kara was more excited than ever for her party.

1 **What color balloons does Kara want at her party?**

a)   blue and green

b)   red and yellow

c)   pink and purple

d)   purple and gold

2 **What is a food pantry?**

a)   a place where people come to find jobs

b)   a place that stores food that people don't have room for

c)   a place people go to get food

d)   a store where people buy food

3 **What is the main idea of the story?**

a)   Kara decides she wants to help others more than she wants to get presents.

b)   Kara decides not to have a birthday party if she can't get presents.

c)   Kara's mother wants her to donate her presents to a charity.

d)   Kara feels bad for having a party.

4 **What do you think Kara will get at her birthday party? Explain why.**

_____

_____

_____

5 **What did Kara's mother do that helped change Kara's mind about her birthday party?**

a)   took her shopping

b)   wrote notes about her party

c)   got food for a food pantry

d)   went to a bank

A   Pretend you are Kara. Write an invitation. Add what you think she wrote about presents.

You're Invited to a Party!

For: _____

Date: _____

When: _____

Where: _____

Please Bring: _____

_____

_____

Please RSVP by phone or email:

Phone Number: _____

Email Address: _____

Name: _____

B   Write a list of healthy foods you would like to bring to a food pantry.

_____   _____

_____   _____

_____   _____

_____   _____

C   Write about a time when you helped someone else by giving.

_____

_____

_____

_____

_____

_____

_____

Name: _____

D Write about what Kara might say to her friends when she gets her gifts.

_____

_____

_____

_____

_____

_____

_____

_____

_____

_____

_____

Unit 7

Learning About . . .
Good Judgment

Teacher Notes

Passage Summary
John has to decide whether to confess that he has not paid attention to the fire safety lesson as he is about to be tested on the skill.

Concepts to Consider
John initially shows bad judgment by not paying attention to the fire safety lesson. However, he redeems himself in the end by admitting he is not prepared to actually light a fire. He also decides to pay attention to future lessons, indicating he has learned a long-term lesson rather than a one-time lesson.

Discussion Questions
- What did John do that showed bad judgment?
- What did John do that showed good judgment?
- Tell about a time when you made a decision that showed good judgment.

"All right, campers," Mrs. Dietz said. "This morning, we are going to learn campfire safety."

John rolled his eyes. Everything at camp was about safety! They had a safety lesson for every activity the kids had done so far. Safe swimming. Safe hiking. Safe boating. John was sick of the word "safety." Wasn't camp supposed to be about having fun?

John acted as if he was listening to Mrs. Dietz. She was explaining how to start a campfire. Was it that hard to figure out? John wondered. He pretended to pay attention.

Just when he thought the safety lesson was over, Mrs. Dietz said, "Now, here is the safe way to put a fire out."

John yawned. "Everybody knows how to put a fire out," he grumbled. "You put water on it."

Finally, the lesson was over. Campers went in groups of two to the fire pits. Adults were there to watch them start and put out a small fire.

Page 1

Good Judgment

John was waiting for his turn. He suddenly felt nervous. He tried to remember what Mrs. Dietz had told them about fires. "I should have paid more attention," he thought.

He looked around the campground. All the other campers looked like they knew what they were doing. It would be embarrassing if he didn't know how to do the job right.

The camper in front of John finished putting out the small fire she had built. John watched as the grown-up said, "Very good job, Amanda."

Now it was John's turn. He swallowed hard. He knew if he messed up, the adults would be there to put out the fire. Still, he knew that he should not try to start a fire without knowing what he was doing.

"What if everyone laughs at me for needing another lesson?" he thought. But being laughed at would be better than doing something he knew was unsafe.

"John," the grown-up said, "are you ready to start your campfire?"

Page 2

John stood still for a moment. Then he shook his head.

"No," he said quietly. "I'm not ready."

"What do you mean?" the grown-up asked.

John hung his head. "I didn't pay attention at the safety lesson. I don't think I should try this until I learn the right way to do it." He wondered if he was in trouble. To his surprise, the grown-up smiled.

"John, thank you for being honest. You are very smart to admit that you need help. That was a good decision," the man said.

John smiled back. He was surprised. No one had laughed. No one was angry. Still, he was going to pay attention at every safety lesson from now on.

Page 3

1 **What does "nervous" mean?**

    a)   careless

    b)   fearful or worried

    c)   quiet

    d)   tired and hungry

2 **Did the other kids listen to the lesson? Why do you think so?**

_____

_____

_____

3 **When Mrs. Dietz was explaining how to light a campfire, how did John feel about it?**

    a)   that it seemed hard

    b)   that Mrs. Dietz didn't know the right way

    c)   that it was easy

    d)   that the other kids were poor listeners

4 **Put the events of the story in order:**   _____ _____ _____ _____

    a)   John admits that he didn't listen to the lesson.

    b)   John goes to camp.

    c)   John gets nervous when it is his turn to make a fire.

    d)   John doesn't listen to the campfire safety lesson.

5 *Fire is hot.* **Is this a fact or an opinion? Explain your answer.**

    a)   fact   b)   opinion

_____

_____

_____

Name: _____

A Pretend you are John. Write a letter to your parents telling about the lesson you learned today.

_____

_____

_____

_____

_____

_____

_____

_____

_____

_____

Name: _____

B Make a list of things that might have happened if John had tried to light a fire without understanding the right way to do it.

_____

_____

_____

_____

_____

C Write a list of safety lessons you might learn at camp.

_____

_____

_____

_____

_____

Name: _____

D Describe a time when you learned a valuable lesson about safety.

_____

_____

_____

_____

_____

_____

_____

_____

_____

_____

_____

Teacher Notes

Passage Summary

Marcus weighs the importance of appearing to get a good grade and actually earning an honest grade. He cheats on a math test and must decide how to face the results. Will he be honest about his dishonesty?

Concepts to Consider

Marcus's dilemma is made worse by the fact that he has memorized the test answers, so he can't change his mind and take the test with honest results. He is left with two courses of action: accept a grade he did not earn, or tell the teacher what has happened. He displays both honest and dishonest characteristics. Collier, his dishonest partner in crime, clearly doesn't believe there is honor among thieves, as he seems certain that Marcus will tell on both of them. Whether Marcus simply admits to his dishonest behavior or implicates Collier is up to the reader to decide.

Discussion Questions

- What do you think will happen to Marcus next?

- If you were Marcus, would you tell Mr. Jessup about Collier?

- What do you think would make Marcus's parents more upset: a bad grade on a test or cheating on a test? Why do you think so?

Honesty

Marcus chewed on his pencil. He looked around the classroom. Everyone else was busy writing the answers on their tests. They would probably get all the right answers, Marcus thought. He was terrible at math. He was terrible at tests.

"I can't get another low score," he said to himself. His parents would be disappointed. Marcus wanted to make them proud, and he had to admit that it would be nice to impress the other kids with a great grade, too.

Mr. Jessup handed the tests back the next day. Marcus was relieved to see he had only missed six problems. He saw that Collier was grinning at a big 100% on his test.

That night Marcus couldn't sleep. The next math test was in two weeks. He wanted to get a better score, and it would be great to surprise his parents with a good grade.

Page 1

How had Collier gotten an A? Last year, Collier usually got Cs or Ds on math tests.

After class, Marcus talked to Collier. "Hey," he said. "I saw your grade. How did you manage to get an A?"

Collier whispered, "I had a little help."

"What do you mean?" Marcus asked.

"My sister had Mr. Jessup last year," Collier said. "She saved all her tests, and Mr. Jessup gives the same ones every year."

"You cheated?" Marcus couldn't believe his ears.

"Shhh!" Collier hissed. "Listen, if you want, I could give you some help on the next test. But you can't tell anyone. It's our little secret."

Page 2

By the following Friday, Marcus had made his decision. Collier slipped him a copy of his sister's old test, and Marcus memorized the answers over the weekend.

Before the test, Collier looked at Marcus and gave him a thumbs-up. Marcus felt sick. It was too late to change his mind—he already knew the answers, so he would be cheating no matter what. Marcus took a deep breath and began working the first problem.

When the bell rang, Collier waited at the door for him. Marcus ignored him and walked up to Mr. Jessup. Collier backed away from the door, and Marcus heard him running down the hall.

"Mr. Jessup, I have something to tell you," Marcus said to his teacher.

Page 3

Name: _____

1 **What is one reason Marcus wanted to get a good grade on his math test?**

a) so the kids would stop teasing him

b) to make his parents proud

c) to make Mr. Jessup proud

d) to get a better grade than Collier

2 **Marcus is *relieved* he missed six problems. What does that mean?**

a) He wished he did better.

b) He thought Mr. Jessup marked it wrong.

c) He knew Collier did better than him.

d) He was glad he didn't do worse.

3 **Did Marcus see his score on the test before talking to Collier or after?**

a) before

b) after

4 **Why do you think Collier runs away?**

a) He doesn't like Marcus.

b) He doesn't want to get caught cheating.

c) He sees his sister.

d) He has to get to gym class.

5 **Is cheating against the rules in Mr. Jessup's class? How do you know?**

_____

_____

_____

_____

Name: _____

A Write a dialog for the conversation that you think Marcus and Mr. Jessup will have.

Marcus: _____

_____

Mr. Jessup: _____

_____

_____

Marcus: _____

_____

_____

Mr. Jessup: _____

_____

_____

Marcus: _____

_____

_____

B Write about what Collier and Marcus might say to each other after Marcus talked to Mr. Jessup.

_____

_____

_____

_____

_____

C Write about a time when you were honest about being dishonest.

_____

_____

_____

_____

_____

Name: _____

D Write about a time when someone was dishonest to you. How did it make you feel? What did you do?

_____

_____

_____

_____

_____

_____

_____

_____

_____

_____

_____

_____

Teacher Notes

Passage Summary

Jenna nearly betrays her best friend by almost telling her friend's secret. She finds that even though she didn't really tell, her friend is so upset at her disloyalty that their friendship might be ruined.

Concepts to Consider

In Mandy's perception, Jenna has betrayed her by merely giving clues about her secret, even though Jenna is too loyal in the end to announce that secret. In Jenna's mind, this last-second loyalty should be enough for Mandy, but when Mandy points out that she would never give hints about Jenna's secrets, Jenna begins to understand that loyalty is about more than big actions—it's sometimes about the little ones. Just by playing along with the secret game, she has put her friendship in jeopardy. Whether the two are loyal enough to remain friends is left undetermined, which can add to the discussion of the character attribute. The reader understands that Jenna wants to remain Mandy's friend, but will Mandy feel enough loyalty to Jenna to forgive her?

Discussion Questions

- Who is the more loyal friend, Jenna or Mandy?

- Do you think Taylor is loyal to her friends? Why do you think so?

- Have you ever told someone else's secret? How did you feel afterward? How did the other person feel?

Loyalty

The slumber party was as much fun as Jenna had hoped it would be. Jenna had been worried when she found out her best friend, Mandy, wasn't going to be there. The other girls were sometimes mean—they liked to gossip and tell secrets about other kids. So far, they weren't acting like that. Jenna was enjoying herself even without Mandy.

"Let's play 'Guess the Secret,'" Taylor suggested. Jenna's heart sank. This didn't sound like a game she wanted to play. The other girls yelled with excitement.

"Okay," Taylor said. "Jenna, here are the rules. You have to think of a secret about someone who's not in the room. You tell us who you're thinking about, and we have to guess the secret. You give us clues until we run out of guesses."

Jenna gulped.

Page 1

"Let's see . . . Mandy's not here," Taylor said. "So think of a secret about her."

Well, that wasn't hard to do. Jenna and Mandy were best friends—they knew lots of secrets about each other.

"Okay," Jenna said.

As the other girls made their guesses, Jenna began to enjoy giving them more clues. Mandy's secret wasn't that bad. If the girls guessed right, Jenna hoped they would forget by Monday.

Finally, Taylor guessed right. Jenna gulped again. Should she admit that Taylor had guessed the secret? Jenna didn't want to lie, but she didn't want to tell Mandy's secret.

Finally, Jenna said, "Nope. You guessed wrong, Taylor." The girls were out of guesses. They moved on to the next secret. Jenna had trouble concentrating. Somehow, she wasn't having fun anymore.

Page 2

On Monday, Jenna and Mandy didn't see each other until lunch. Mandy marched up to the table. Jenna saw that she looked upset.

"Did you tell my secret?" Mandy asked. "The other girls said they tried to guess something about me. They said you gave them clues."

"I didn't tell," Jenna said. She felt like crying. Why had she even played along with the other girls?

"But you used my secret for the game. You gave them clues to help them guess," Mandy said. "I wouldn't have done that to you."

Mandy walked off and sat with some other girls. Jenna looked down at the table. She hadn't really told the secret, but she felt terrible anyway. She wondered what she could do to make it up to Mandy. She hoped she hadn't lost her best friend over a stupid game.

Page 3

❶ What does the word "admit" mean in this story?

    a)   to tell someone you did something

    b)   to let someone play with you

❷ How do you play "Guess the Secret"?

_____

_____

_____

_____

_____

❸ How does Jenna feel when the girls decide to play "Guess the Secret"?

    a)   uncomfortable

    b)   excited

    c)   angry

    d)   sad

❹ True or false? Taylor guessed Mandy's secret.

    a)   true

    b)   false

❺ Why did Jenna feel bad when she talked to Mandy?

    a)   Mandy wanted to be best friends with Taylor.

    b)   The other girls didn't like her anymore.

    c)   She felt that Mandy was upset over nothing.

    d)   She felt she had been disloyal by giving clues about Mandy's secret.

Name: _____

A Finish the story by writing a conversation Mandy and Jenna might have after school.

_____

_____

_____

_____

_____

_____

_____

_____

_____

_____

_____

B Pretend you are Mandy. Write a note to Jenna to tell her how you feel.

_____

_____

_____

_____

_____

_____

_____

_____

C How could Jenna show Mandy how sorry she is?

_____

_____

_____

_____

Name: _____

D Pretend you are Jenna. Write a letter to Mandy to tell her how you feel.

Teacher Notes

Passage Summary

Maria and her family attend a Memorial Day parade, and she learns about what it means to honor those who serve their country.

Concepts to Consider

A parade is always exciting to children, and they associate it with fun. However, a Memorial Day parade is a good time to help them explore the concept of patriotism. The example of soldiers, both active and retired, whose patriotism is tangible, provides an opportunity for adults to show that love of one's country is not shown by waving the flag or reciting the pledge, but by understanding duty, loyalty, and appreciation.

Discussion Questions

- What was the purpose of the parade Maria's family attended?

- How do you think Maria felt when the soldiers marched by?

- Tell about a time when you learned something about the United States.

Patriotism

Maria hurried to keep up with her family. They'd parked very far away from where the parade was going to start. Her father was afraid they would miss the beginning.

"Let's go," he called to the kids. "We don't have much time."

It seemed like everyone on the street was holding a little American flag. Maria wondered where they had gotten them. Then she saw a woman handing them out.

"Can we get flags?" she asked.

"Sure," Mom said. She went over to the woman and came back with four flags, one for everyone in the family.

"Let's find a place to stand," Dad said. "The parade is about to start."

They found an open spot, right by the street. Even Maria's little brother would be able to see because they were in front.

Page 1

"Who are they?" Maria asked. She pointed to the people who were waiting to march. There were men and women. They all had uniforms on. Some people had medals pinned to their uniforms.

"They are in the military," her mother said. "Some are in the Army. Some are in the Navy. Some are in the Air Force. And the ones closest to us are Marines."

"What is 'military'?" Maria's little brother asked.

Maria was glad that he had asked. She didn't know the answer.

"Those people have a job, and it is to protect the United States," her father said. "They have made a decision to work for their country, and even to fight for it."

"Like if there is a war?" Maria asked.

"Exactly," said her mother. "And when there is not a war, they work to keep things peaceful."

Page 2

Maria looked at the soldiers again. They were lined up in straight rows. They looked very serious. Some held flags that were much bigger than the one she had in her hand.

"Why are some of them old and some of them young?" she asked.

"The older ones fought in wars a long time ago," her father answered. "The younger ones are working now for the country."

"Why are they in the parade?" Maria's little brother wondered.

"This parade is to help us remember all the soldiers who have died in wars," Mom said. "Every year, we have a holiday called Memorial Day. We take time to show respect and thankfulness for soldiers."

Maria was about to ask a question, but the siren went off. The parade was starting. She waved her flag and watched as the soldiers marched by. She stood straight and tall, just like them.

Page 3

Name: _____

1 **What is another word for "soldiers"?**

   a)   members of the military

   b)   parade-goers

   c)   family

   d)   company

2 **What do Maria and her brother get at the parade?**

   a)   candy

   b)   toy cars

   c)   American flags

   d)   kites

3 **What do you think Maria will do with her flag after the parade?**

   _____

   _____

   _____

4 **Who does Maria go to the parade with?**

   a)   her grandparents

   b)   her mom, dad, and little sister

   c)   her mom, dad, and little brother

   d)   soldiers

5 **Put the events of the story in order:**   _____ _____ _____ _____

   a)   get flags

   b)   hear the siren

   c)   park the car

   d)   walk to the parade

Name: _____

A Write a letter to a soldier to thank him or her for keeping your country safe. Use the space below to write what you might say.

_____

_____

_____

_____

_____

_____

_____

_____

_____

_____

_____

Name: _____

B Pretend you are Maria. What would you say to a soldier after the parade?

_____

_____

_____

_____

_____

C Make a list of times when you think, talk, or sing about your country.

_____

_____

_____

_____

_____

Name: _____

D Write an acrostic poem about what you think it means to be patriotic. Write a word or phrase related to patriotism on each line. Make sure each line begins with the correct letter in the word "PATRIOTIC" as marked.

P _____

A _____

T _____

R _____

I _____

O _____

T _____

I _____

C _____

Unit 11

Perseverance

Teacher Notes

Passage Summary

Leah wants to give up karate lessons because she has trouble keeping up with the more experienced students, but she makes a commitment to herself to keep trying to attain her goal of a yellow belt.

Concepts to Consider

Leah's story focuses on the actual choice to persevere, rather than the results of perseverance. Whether or not Leah attains her yellow belt is not revealed in the story. Instead, the conclusion focuses on Leah's continued determination to work as hard as she is able to achieve her goal. Failure is only failure when one stops trying altogether, and conversely, success does not mean that one should stop setting goals. There is satisfaction in trying your hardest to achieve a goal, even if the goal is not attained at that time.

Discussion Questions

- What choices did Leah have about going to karate class?

- What are some activities you've had trouble doing because you were new at them?

- How do you think Leah will feel if she doesn't earn a yellow belt at her first testing?

- If Leah earns a yellow belt, do you think she will then quit karate?

- Who helps Leah most with her karate: her teacher, her mother, or Leah herself? Why do you think so?

Perseverance

Leah sighed and put on her uniform. She was unhappy. At her last karate lesson, the older kids had made fun of her. Leah was new at karate, and she did not always understand what the sensei, or teacher, was saying. She had trouble with the moves, especially the kicks.

"I do not want to go," Leah said to herself. She tied her white belt tighter around her waist. She tried to think about what it would feel like to earn a yellow belt. That would mean she was getting better at karate.

"Let's go!" her mother called. Leah walked to the car. She decided she would work hard to learn today's lesson. Each little move that Leah got right would bring her closer to that yellow belt.

During the lesson, Leah kept her eyes on the sensei. She worked hard to imitate the moves. She did not look at, or listen to, the other students. She just focused on her own feet and hands.

Page 1

At the end of the lesson, Sensei Nelson called her over.

"You did a very good job today," Sensei Nelson said. "You did not give up trying to follow the lesson. If you would like extra practice, I would be happy to help you after class."

"I'll ask my mom," Leah said. Her mom thought it was a great idea, and Leah began to work harder than ever to learn the karate moves. Soon, Sensei Nelson told her she was ready to try for her yellow belt.

On the day of the test, Leah tied her white belt around her waist. She hoped it would be the last time she used that belt. Would she have a yellow belt by the end of the day?

When she got to the gym, other kids were practicing. They all looked nervous. Leah was nervous, too. Part of her wanted to go home, but she had worked too hard to give up now.

Page 2

Perseverance

When they called her name, Leah walked onto the mat. Her sensei and her mom gave her big smiles. Leah took a deep breath. She would try her very hardest, and if she did not get her yellow belt this time, she would not give up. Leah would take the test again and again until she earned that yellow belt. It might take more than one try, but Leah knew she could do it.

Page 3

Name: _____

1 **What color belt does Leah have at the beginning of the story? What color belt does she have when the story ends?**

Beginning of the story: _____

End of the story: _____

2 *You need to take a test to get a yellow belt in karate.* **Is this a fact or an opinion? Explain your answer.**

a) fact   b) opinion

_____

_____

3 **Put the events of the story in order:** _____   _____   _____   _____

a) Leah goes to the karate test.

b) Leah gets help from Sensei Nelson.

c) Leah does not want to go to karate class.

d) Leah decides to focus on her karate lesson.

4 **Does Sensei Nelson want Leah to get a yellow belt? How do you know?**

_____

_____

5 **What did Leah do after Sensei Nelson offered her extra help?**

a) took her test for her yellow belt

b) asked her mom if it was okay to take extra lessons

c) tied her white belt around her waist

d) gave up

Name: _____

A Write two endings for the story. In one, Leah earns her yellow belt. In the second ending, Leah does not earn her yellow belt. Explain how she feels in each story and what she decides to do.

Ending 1—Leah earns her yellow belt.

_____

_____

_____

_____

_____

Ending 2—No yellow belt this time.

_____

_____

_____

_____

_____

Name: _____

B List two ways Leah could help another karate student who wants to give up.

1 _____

_____

_____

2 _____

_____

_____

C What do you think will happen when Leah earns her yellow belt? Will she stop taking karate? Will she continue?

_____

_____

_____

_____

_____

Name: _____

D Write about a time when you wanted to give up but did not. Explain how and why you persevered.

_____

_____

_____

_____

_____

_____

_____

_____

_____

_____

_____

Teacher Notes

Passage Summary

Christy laughs as her class makes fun of a substitute teacher and later comes to realize that even passive participation in such behavior shows disrespect.

Concepts to Consider

Christy believes she has not contributed to the atmosphere of disrespect in her classroom because she did not overtly make fun of the substitute. However, her parents point out to her that laughing at and egging on the other children is just as disrespectful as outright mockery. The lesson is driven home by Christy's mother's anecdote of her first teaching experience. Christy's parents help her understand that the attitude of respect should come from understanding and empathy, rather than simply lip service to the character attribute. The story ends ambiguously, but hints that Christy is considering her mother's experience as she weighs her answer to her father's question.

Discussion Questions

- Who acted disrespectfully?
- Were the students who laughed just as disrespectful as the students who made fun of the substitute?
- Tell about a time someone made fun of you for something. How did it make you feel?

Respect

Christy knew she should not laugh, but she could not help it. The other kids were so funny! Mr. Jefferson, the substitute teacher, was getting angry. The kids in Christy's class were making fun of the way he talked.

"That's enough!" Mr. Jefferson yelled. Rory, who sat next to Christy, said, "That's enough!" in a silly voice that sounded a lot like Mr. Jefferson's.

The substitute teacher threw his hands up in the air. "Didn't anyone ever teach you kids to respect your teachers?"

Christy looked around at her classmates. They knew very well that they were supposed to treat teachers with respect. Somehow, though, when Ms. Pennington was out sick, the kids seemed to forget that lesson.

Christy's mom was a substitute teacher, but she only taught older kids. Christy wondered what she would do if her classes acted like this one.

Page 1

Mr. Jefferson passed out the quiz on state capitals. "Use pencils, not pens, on this quiz," he said. This time, two of the kids made fun of his voice at the same time. Christy giggled again. Then she said to Rory, "You do his voice best. Say something else."

"I'm a big dummy," Rory said in his silly voice. The classroom exploded with laughter.

That night, Christy told her parents about Mr. Jefferson's trouble in her class. She was surprised when both of her parents were angry with her.

"You should not have acted like that," her mom said.

"But I didn't make fun of him!" Christy said. "I only laughed."

"You told Rory to keep making fun of him," her father said. "And laughing at Mr. Jefferson was just as disrespectful as making fun of him."

Her mother sighed. "I remember the first time I taught," she said. "The students made fun of me for the whole day."

Page 2

"Why?" Christy said. Her mom was a great teacher! Christy felt angry that kids would make fun of her.

"Because I am short," her mother explained. "Some of the students were taller than me. They thought it was a big joke. They put some of the papers I needed on a high shelf. I couldn't get them down by myself. I had to stand on a chair."

Christy thought about Mr. Jefferson. It wasn't his fault his voice was different. She wondered how it felt to have a bunch of kids making fun of something you couldn't change.

"Is Mr. Jefferson teaching again tomorrow?" her mother asked.

"Yes," Christy said.

"Will you treat him with respect?" her father asked.

Christy thought about it. She knew tomorrow was going to be different.

Page 3

Name: _____

1 **What did the kids make fun of Mr. Jefferson about?**

a) his voice

b) his hair

c) his height

d) his clothes

2 **How do you think Christy will answer her father's question at the end of the story?**

_____

_____

_____

3 **Put the events of the story in order:** _____ _____ _____ _____

a) Christy's parents get angry with her.

b) Rory makes fun of Mr. Jefferson's voice.

c) Christy's father asks her if she will treat Mr. Jefferson with respect.

d) Christy's mother tells a story.

4 **What is another word for "silly"?**

a) quiet

b) hungry

c) happy

d) goofy

5 **Christy's mother's story was about a time**

a) she made fun of a teacher.

b) kids made fun of her.

c) Christy made fun of her.

d) Christy got in trouble.

Name: _____

A Write an ending to the story about respect.

The next day _____

_____

_____

_____

_____

_____

_____

_____

_____

_____

_____

Name: _____

B Use the space below to list ways you can show respect for teachers.

I show respect by _____

_____

_____

_____

_____

C Use the space below to list ways you can show respect for your friends and classmates.

I show respect by _____

_____

_____

_____

_____

D Pretend you are a student in Mr. Jefferson's class. Write an apology letter to him. Explain how you will be more respectful in the future.

_____

_____

_____

_____

_____

_____

_____

_____

_____

_____

Teacher Notes

Passage Summary

Jason and his brother Mac have different attitudes toward being responsible for packing camping gear, and the results reflect their attitudes.

Concepts to Consider

It is implied that Mac is too careless and irresponsible to pack his life jacket, so if Jason doesn't tell him, Mac will miss his favorite activity. Although Jason is willing to help him, Mac resents having to work toward a goal, and his half-hearted attempts at packing are in contrast with Jason's methodical approach. Jason's efforts will be rewarded, because he has taken the time to do his work in order to have his fun. Mac only wants all the benefits of work, but none of the liabilities. Also note that the boys' parents give them the opportunity to show responsibility, rather than doing the work for them.

Discussion Questions

- What did Jason do that showed responsibility?

- What did Mac's behavior show?

- Who will Mac and Jason's parents be more proud of? Why do you think so?

It was almost time for the Martin family camping trip. Jason and his twin brother, Mac, couldn't wait! The family was going to leave right after the last day of school ended. Mom and Dad were going to pick the boys up right outside of school.

Jason smiled. The other kids would be jealous when they saw the canoe on the roof of the car. The Martins loved to put their life jackets on and go for a ride down the river. Canoeing was the boys' favorite part of the trip.

The day before the trip, Dad said, "You boys are old enough to help this year. You'll be in charge of packing the things you will need."

"That's easy," Mac said. "Sleeping bags, clothes, and hiking boots."

"And your life jackets, soap, toothpaste, and a lot of other things," Mom added.

"Mom, can we make our own lists?" Jason said. "You and Dad can look at them and tell us if we missed something."

Page 1

"Okay," Mom agreed.

As they sat down to write their lists, Mac complained. "Why did you say we would do this?" he asked Jason. "I like it when Mom and Dad make the lists and pack for us."

"I'll help you," Jason promised. The boys wrote down everything they thought they might need.

Mom looked at their lists. "You did a good job," she said. "Now, you have to pack everything you wrote down, and put your bags by the front door when you are finished."

"This stinks," Mac complained. "All the other kids are outside playing, and we have to work. It's not fair."

Page 2

Jason shook his head. Why didn't Mac just pack, instead of complaining about it?

"I'll help you again," he said to Mac.

"No way," Mac said. "I can do it myself. Let's just get it over with so we can have some fun."

The boys went to their rooms to fill their bags. Jason took his list along, and each time he packed an item, he crossed it off the list. When he was finished in his room, he went to the garage. He packed his life jacket and crossed it off the list. He waited for Mac to come out and get his life jacket, too.

Mac never came out to the garage. Jason went inside and saw Mac's bag by the front door. Then he noticed Mac's list. It was still on the table, right where Mac had sat down to write it.

"Did you use your list to pack?" Jason asked Mac.

"Oh, who needs it?" Mac said. "I remembered everything."

Page 3

1 **Put the events of the story in order.** _____ _____ _____ _____

    a)   Jason sees Mac's life jacket in the garage.

    b)   Jason and Mac make lists.

    c)   Jason uses his list to pack.

    d)   Mom and Dad check the lists.

2 **What did the boys pack their things in?**

    a)   suitcases

    b)   boxes

    c)   bags

    d)   trunks

3 **When is the family leaving on their camping trip?**

    a)   right after school ends

    b)   at the end of the summer

    c)   the day before school ends

    d)   Fourth of July

4 **How did Jason pack differently than Mac did?**

_____

_____

_____

5 **Do you think Jason will remind Mac about his life jacket?**   YES   NO
Explain your answer.

_____

_____

_____

Name: _____

A Pretend you are going on a camping trip. Write a list of things you will need to take with you.

My Camping Trip List

1 _____

2 _____

3 _____

4 _____

5 _____

6 _____

7 _____

8 _____

9 _____

10 _____

11 _____

12 _____

13 _____

14 _____

**Unit 13: Responsibility
Writing Activities**

Name: _____

B If you were Jason, would you tell Mac he forgot to pack his life jacket? Why or why not?

_____

_____

_____

_____

_____

C How do you think Mac will feel if he gets to the campsite and realizes he forgot his life jacket?

_____

_____

_____

_____

_____

Name: _____

D Write about a time when you acted responsibly.

_____

_____

_____

_____

_____

_____

_____

_____

_____

_____

_____

Teacher Notes

Passage Summary

Kevin, the new kid in class, is teased about his accent. His classmate Jorge has a discussion with him that teaches both boys about tolerating differences amongst people.

Concepts to Consider

Children may tend to seize upon overt differences as ways to ostracize others. This tendency to make someone else feel bad in order to make oneself feel better is just as destructive as intolerance due to prejudice. The attribute of tolerance might best be described as "accepting others' differences." Another good way of teaching children tolerance is reminding them of the Golden Rule—treat others as you would like to be treated yourself. In fact, the word "tolerance" is somewhat loaded: it implies that accepting others is somehow a burden and implies a value judgment. Perhaps a better way to think of this character attribute is "I respect each individual and accept others' differences."

Discussion Questions

- How do you think the kids felt when they teased Kevin?
- Why do you think Jorge stopped laughing at Kevin?
- How do you think Kevin felt in class?

"Ms. Ryan, can I borrow a pencil?" Kevin asked.

The other kids all giggled. Kevin talked so differently! He was new to the class—in fact, he was new to the United States. His family had moved from Ireland, and they all sounded different when they talked.

Kevin looked down at his desk. His ears were bright red. Jorge stopped laughing with the other kids. He remembered when he had just moved to the United States. He couldn't speak English very well. Some of the kids had teased him. Jorge had been sad every day.

Now, Jorge spoke English very well. But some of his family still got teased for the way they talked.

At lunch, Jorge walked over to Kevin. He was sitting by himself, watching the other kids play soccer outside.

"Do you like to play soccer?" he asked Kevin.

Page 1

Kevin looked away. "You better not talk to me," he said quietly. "The other kids will tease you."

Jorge sat down next to Kevin. "I know what it's like to be teased," he said. "I don't care if they do."

Kevin smiled. "I wish I didn't talk like this. Maybe I should try to learn how everyone talks in the United States. I could copy the way they talk. Then no one can make fun of me."

Jorge shrugged. "But not everyone in the United States talks the same. In fact, not everyone in our class talks the same."

"What do you mean?" Kevin asked.

"Well, for instance, I have an accent because I learned to speak Spanish before English," Jorge explained. "Mandy can't say the letter 's' very well. Derrick lived down South before, so he has a Southern accent. Allen stutters—sometimes the words get stuck in his mouth."

Page 2

"Wow," Kevin said. He thought for a moment. "But if everyone talks differently, then why am I the only one who gets teased?"

Now it was Jorge's turn to think. Finally he answered, "I guess it's because you are new and people aren't used to the way you talk. Someday, we won't even notice anymore."

"Or maybe I'll learn to talk like someone else in class, so no one will tease me," Kevin said. "I bet I could learn fast."

"No," Jorge said slowly. "I think you should just be yourself. Besides, it's kind of cool to hear all the different ways people talk, don't you think?"

"Maybe you're right," Kevin said. A smile spread slowly across his face. "Or maybe I could teach you all to talk the way I do."

Jorge laughed. It would be funny to hear that!

Page 3

1 **Why do the kids tease Kevin?**

a)   He talks with a lisp.

b)   He stutters when he talks.

c)   He can't play soccer.

d)   He has an Irish accent.

2 **Why do you think Jorge started talking to Kevin?**

a)   He wanted to learn about Ireland.

b)   He knew how it felt to get teased.

c)   He wanted him to play soccer.

d)   He wanted to make fun of him.

3 **Do you think Kevin will change the way he talks? Why or why not?**

_____

_____

4 **Do you think Kevin felt better or worse after Jorge talked with him? Why do you think so?**

_____

_____

5 **What are some of the ways the kids talked differently in the class?**

_____

_____

_____

_____

Name: _____

A Write about something that makes you different from other people.

_____

_____

_____

_____

_____

_____

_____

_____

_____

_____

_____

_____

Name: _____

B   Write a list of things that you have in common with kids in your class.

_____

_____

_____

_____

_____

C   Write a paragraph or a poem about what it feels like to be teased.

_____

_____

_____

_____

_____

Name: _____

D Pretend you are Kevin, and write a letter to someone in Ireland to talk about school in the United States.

_____

_____

_____

_____

_____

_____

_____

_____

_____

_____

Teacher Notes

Passage Summary

Sacagawea played a vital role in the Lewis and Clark expedition. Because of her trustworthiness, she was a respected part of the group.

Concepts to Consider

Sacagawea is a strong role model for many reasons, not the least of which is her trustworthiness. By helping Lewis and Clark in every way she could, she earned their trust. She further proved her honesty and trustworthiness by stopping others from taking advantage of Lewis and Clark. No doubt she had to earn the trust of people on both sides of the communication gap, and it speaks to her honor that this trust was given so readily. Sacagawea's trustworthiness was a big part of the success of Lewis and Clark's journey.

Discussion Questions

- In what ways did Lewis and Clark trust Sacagawea?
- Do you think Sacagawea liked exploring with the group? Why or why not?
- Tell about a time when someone trusted you with an important job.

A long time ago, two men named Lewis and Clark were asked to do an important job. The president asked them to explore a new part of the country. Exploring was dangerous back then. The men needed all the help they could get.

The men knew they would meet Native Americans along the way. Lewis and Clark wanted to be able to talk with them. They were worried about this. They didn't speak the Native Americans' languages. They knew they needed help.

Lewis and Clark needed a person they could trust. They wanted to tell this person what to say to the Native Americans. Then they needed to know what the people said back.

They decided to ask a native woman to help them. Her name was Sacagawea. She spoke two languages. She could talk to the Native Americans. She would tell them what Lewis and Clark said. Then she would tell Lewis and Clark what the Native Americans said.

Page 1

Trustworthiness

Sacagawea agreed to leave her home and help Lewis and Clark. It must have been hard to go with strangers. Still, she went. She knew it was an important job.

Sacagawea did a good job helping Lewis and Clark. She didn't just help them speak with the Native Americans they met. She knew a lot about plants and animals, and she helped the explorers find food. At least once, she saved their supplies when their boat tipped over in a river. Sacagawea helped Lewis and Clark find the best trails through the mountains.

Page 2

Because she was such a big help to them, Lewis and Clark trusted Sacagawea more every day. They knew she was an important part of their group.

For one part of their trip, Lewis and Clark needed horses and food. Some Native Americans agreed to sell them both, but Sacagawea found out these Native Americans were lying. They were not going to give them the horses, and they were going to leave Lewis and Clark instead of helping them. Sacagawea told Lewis and Clark. They asked her to help again. She went to the people and got them to agree to sell the horses.

The Native Americans and Lewis and Clark all trusted that Sacagawea was telling them the truth. They knew she was honest. Because of her help, Lewis and Clark did their job and explored a new part of the country.

Page 3

1 **Name two ways Sacagawea helped Lewis and Clark.**

_____

_____

_____

2 **What is another word for "dangerous"?**

a) mountainous

b) risky

c) hard

d) uneven

3 *Exploring is fun.* **Is this a fact or an opinion? Explain your answer.**

a) fact   b) opinion

_____

_____

4 **Why did Lewis and Clark go exploring?**

a) to find diamonds

b) to look for horses

c) to find out about new parts of the country

d) to find Sacagawea

5 **What did Lewis and Clark want to buy from the Native Americans?**

a) cows and food

b) a new boat and food

c) horses and maps

d) horses and food

Name: _____

A Imagine you are Sacagawea. Write a diary entry about a day in your journey with Lewis and Clark.

Dear Diary,

_____

_____

_____

_____

_____

_____

_____

_____

_____

_____

Name: _____

B Write about a time when you did not trust someone.

_____

_____

_____

_____

_____

C Write about a time when someone did not trust you. How did it make you feel?

_____

_____

_____

_____

_____

Name: _____

D Pretend you are going exploring. Write about three people you would trust to take on your journey. Explain why you would invite each person.

Person 1: _____

_____

_____

_____

Person 2: _____

_____

_____

_____

Person 3: _____

_____

_____

_____

Suggested Answers for Reading Comprehension Questions

Page 9

1. a, c
2. a
3. b
4. b
5. They like her. Reasons will vary.

Page 17

1. c
2. Answers include fed, clothed, and sheltered people, and helped them when they were sick.
3. b, false—Mother Teresa did not have children of her own.
4. a
5. c

Page 25

1. b, c
2. b—Answers will vary.
3. Yes—Answers will vary.
4. c
5. b, d, a, c

Page 33

1. d
2. c
3. b
4. a
5. a—The law was changed.

Page 41

1. d
2. right to vote
   equal pay
   equal jobs
   equal schools

3. *Possible answers:*
   had meetings
   made speeches
   talked to family and friends
   marched
4. b—Answers will vary.
5. Answers will vary. *Possible answer:*
   The women convinced others to see that men and women were both smart and able to work and could choose good people when they voted.

Page 49

1. b
2. c
3. a
4. Food for the food pantry to help others.
5. c

Page 57

1. b
2. Answers will vary. Other kids seemed to have listened since they understood the lesson and the safety rules and were able to make and put out small fires.
3. c
4. b, d, c, a
5. a—Fire burns and is dangerous.

Page 65

1. b
2. d
3. a
4. b
5. Answers will vary. Some answers might include these facts:
   Collier gets upset when Marcus asks if he cheated.
   Marcus debates about seeing the test before he takes it.
   Collier runs away when Marcus asks to speak to Mr. Jessup.

Suggested Answers for Reading Comprehension Questions *(cont.)*

Page 73

1. a
2. Think of a secret about someone who is not in the room.

   Give players clues.

   Players take turns guessing what the secret might be.

   A player guesses the secret.
3. a
4. a
5. d

Page 81

1. a
2. c
3. Opinions will vary.
4. c
5. c, d, a, b

Page 89

1. Beginning: white

   End: white—We don't know how she did on her test.
2. a—The passage states that Leah needs to take a test.
3. c, d, b, a
4. Yes—He offers extra help.
5. b

Page 97

1. a
2. Answers will vary.
3. b, a, d, c
4. d
5. b

Page 105

1. b, d, c, a
2. c
3. a
4. Answers will vary. *Possible answer:*

   Jason packed using his list. Mac did not use a list and forgot things.
5. Answers will vary.

Page 113

1. d
2. b
3. Answers will vary.
4. Answers will vary.
5. lisp

   Southern accent

   Spanish accent

   stutter

Page 121

1. helped find food

   saved supplies

   talked to other Native Americans
2. b
3. b—Reasons will vary.
4. c
5. d

Common Core State Standards Correlation—Grade 2

Each unit in *Reading and Writing Activities for Social-Emotional Learning* meets the following Common Core State Standards © Copyright 2010. Page numbers are provided below for the reading and writing activities. National Governors Association Center for Best Practices and Council of Chief State School Officers. All rights reserved. For more information about the Common Core State Standards, go to *http://www.corestandards.org/*.

English Language Arts/Literacy Standards	
Reading: Literature—Key Ideas and Details	**Page Numbers**
2.RL.2.1 Ask and answer such questions as *who, what, where, when, why*, and *how* to demonstrate understanding of key details in a text.	9, 25, 49, 57, 65, 73, 81, 89, 97, 105, 113
2.RL.2.2 Recount stories, including fables and folktales from diverse cultures, and determine their central message, lesson, or moral.	9, 25, 49, 98
2.RL.2.3 Describe how characters in a story respond to major events and challenges.	11, 52, 75, 100, 105, 107
Reading: Informational Text—Key Ideas and Details	
2.RI.2.1 Ask and answer such questions as *who, what, where, when, why*, and *how* to demonstrate understanding of key details in a text.	17, 33, 41, 121
Reading: Informational Text—Craft and Structure	
2.RI.2.4 Determine the meaning of words and phrases in a text relevant to a *grade 2 topic or subject area.*	9, 17, 33, 41, 49, 57, 73, 81, 97, 121
2.RI.2.6 Identify the main purpose of a text, including what the author wants to answer, explain, or describe.	33, 41
English Language Arts/Writing Standards	
2.W.2.1 Write opinion pieces in which they introduce the topic or book they are writing about, state an opinion, supply reasons that support the opinion, use linking words (e.g., *because, and, also*) to connect opinion and reasons, and provide a concluding statement or section.	11–12, 25, 33, 41–42, 44, 49, 52, 57, 59, 74–76, 81, 90–92, 97, 105, 107
2.W.2.2 Write informative/explanatory texts in which they introduce a topic, use facts and definitions to develop points, and provide a concluding statement or section.	27–28, 34, 42, 51, 58, 65, 74, 82
2.W.2.3 Write narratives in which they recount a well-elaborated event or short sequence of events, include details to describe actions, thoughts, and feelings, use temporal words to signal event order, and provide a sense of closure.	10, 18–20, 26, 34–36, 43, 51–52, 58, 60, 67–68, 75, 83, 92, 98, 100, 108, 115, 122–123

Common Core State Standards Correlation—Grade 3

Each unit in *Reading and Writing Activities for Social-Emotional Learning* meets the following Common Core State Standards © Copyright 2010. Page numbers are provided below for the reading and writing activities. National Governors Association Center for Best Practices and Council of Chief State School Officers. All rights reserved. For more information about the Common Core State Standards, go to *http://www.corestandards.org/*.

English Language Arts/Literacy Standards	
Reading: Literature—Key Ideas and Details	**Page Numbers**
3.RL.3.1 Ask and answer questions to demonstrate understanding of a text, referring explicitly to the text as the basis for the answers.	9, 25, 49, 57, 65, 73, 81, 89, 97, 105, 113
3.RL.3.2 Recount stories, including fables, folktales, and myths from diverse cultures; determine the central message, lesson, or moral and explain how it is conveyed through key details in the text.	9, 25, 49, 98
3.RL.3.2 Describe characters in a story (e.g., their traits, motivations, or feelings) and explain how their actions contribute to the sequence of events.	52, 100, 105, 107
Reading: Informational Text—Key Ideas and Details	
3.RI.3.1 Ask and answer questions to demonstrate understanding of a text, referring explicitly to the text as the basis for the answers.	17, 33, 41, 121
Reading: Informational Text—Craft and Structure	
3.RI.3.4 Determine the meaning of general academic and domain-specific words and phrases in a text relevant to a *grade 3 topic or subject area*.	9, 17, 33, 41, 49, 57, 73, 81, 97, 121
3.RI.3.6 Distinguish their own point of view from that of the author of a text.	33, 41
English Language Arts/Writing Standards	
3.W.3.1 Write opinion pieces on topics or texts, supporting a point of view with reasons.	11–12, 25, 33, 41–42, 44, 49, 52, 57, 59, 74–76, 81, 90–92, 97, 105, 107
3.W.3.2 Write informative/explanatory texts to examine a topic and convey ideas and information clearly.	17, 27–28, 34, 42, 51, 58–59, 65, 74, 82, 99, 113, 124
3.W.3.3 Write narratives to develop real or imagined experiences or events using effective technique, descriptive details, and clear event sequences.	10, 18–20, 26, 34–36, 43, 51–52, 58, 60, 67–68, 75, 90–92, 98, 100, 108, 114–115, 122–124